The Road to ISO 14000

D0366570

The Road to ISO 14000

Glenn K. Nestel
Joseph E. DelRossi
Andrew L. Ullman
Krishnan Rajusrkv
James A. Fava

IRWIN
Professional Publishing®
Chicago • London • Singapore

© Richard D.Irwin, a Times Mirror Higher Education Group, Inc. company, 1996

All rights reserved. No part of this publication may be
reproduced, stored in a retrieval system, or transmitted,
in any form or by any means, electronic, mechanical,
photocopying, recording, or otherwise, without the prior
written permission of the publisher.

This publication is designed to provide accurate and
authoritative information in regard to the subject matter
covered. It is sold with the understanding that neither the
author nor the publisher is engaged in rendering legal, accounting,
or other professional service. If legal advice or other expert
assistance is required, the services of a competent professional
person should be sought.

*From a Declaration of Principles jointly adopted by a Committee
of the American Bar Association and a Committee of Publishers.*

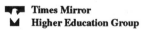

Times Mirror
Higher Education Group

ISBN: 0-7863-0866-4
Library of Congress Catalog Number 95–51289
Printed in the United States of America
1 2 3 4 5 6 7 8 9 0 ML 3 2 1 0 9 8 7 6

Preface

Reasons for Development

In 1991, the International Organization for Standardization (ISO) formed the Strategic Advisory Group on the Environment (SAGE) with a charter to study and make recommendations on the need for international environmental standards. In March 1993, after two years of study, ISO formed Technical Committee 207 and began developing the ISO 14000 series of environmental standards.

Interest in developing the ISO 14000 standards was driven by both the world's changing political landscape and the realities of international trade. The rapidly expanding economies of the European Union, the Pacific Rim, and South America all called for the development of international standards to meet the business strategies of the global marketplace. The success of the ISO 9000 series of quality management standards helped raise the awareness that international standards can be powerful and effective tools to facilitate international trade.

In addition, environmental protection and overall global ecology is having an increased impact on global economic development and international trade. The implications of providing basic human needs (food, shelter, jobs) for an exponentially growing human population (10 billion people by 2025) are staggering. How can third world countries develop their economies and provide for basic needs while maintaining clean air and water and effectively managing their natural resources? What can be done to assure that 21st century economic development and population growth are sustainable and do not exceed the earth's restorative capacity? What are the financial and environmental consequences of increasing energy demands on nonrenewable fossil fuel reserves?

These questions have company-specific implications. How does a company maintain awareness of and comply with the proliferation of country-specific and regional environmental statutes and regulations? How will multinational corporations deal with multilingual, burdensome, and often redundant, conflicting compliance requirements — along with increased environment-related legal liabilities associated with their operations, products, and services? What can be done to prevent environmental issues from becoming defacto free-trade bariers?

ISO 14000 is designed to help companies set up a framework to address these questions effectively without compromising their competitiveness in the gloval economy.

What You Will Learn from Reading This Book

More than 50 ISO member countries now participate in the development of the ISO 14000 series of standards. Worldwide interest in the development of these standards is high, but few people understand the overall context of the standard. *The Road to ISO 14000* provides a general overview of the standard. The book is written in an easy-to-read question-and-answer format and will help you begin your journey to reduce the environmental impacts of your company's activities, products, and services.

Acknowledgments

About the Authors

This book was written by the Management Systems Division of Roy F. Weston, Inc. Primary authors include Joseph DelRossi, division marketing director; Andrew Ullman, project manager and Management Consulting Group leader; Krishnan Rajusrkv, consulting associate; and Glenn Nestel, lead project director and vice-president, Management Systems Division.

We also acknowledge the contributions of James A. Fava, Ph.D., director of the Product Stewardship Practice in WESTON's Management Consulting Division, and Frank Consoli, an

vii

independent consultant and associate of WESTON's Management Systems Division. Jim chairs the U.S. SubTAG for Life Cycle Assessment and is active on the TC 207 LCA Subcommittee. Frank chairs one of the TC 207 Life Cycle Assessment Subcommittee working groups.

About Roy F. Weston, Inc.

Roy F. Weston, Inc. (WESTON®) has been providing environmental consulting, engineering, construction, and analytical services to clients for over 38 years. Founded in 1957, WESTON has a broad client base in the industrial, utility, commercial, and services sectors as well as with local, state, and federal government agencies. The 2,800 employees deployed throughout various divisions and companies can deliver a full range of environmental services capabilities to clients worldwide.

The authors of this book are all from WESTON's Management Systems Division. The Management Systems Division was formed in 1993 to meet a growing demand for management consulting and information management systems services to help clients improve the environmental performance of their operations, products, and services and handle environmental information more efficiently. These services include ISO 14000–related consulting, which helps clients to develop and employ effective environmental management systems.

Contents

Preface   v

Chapter 1
Introduction   1

   Why Is There a Need to Develop National and International
   Environmental Management Standards?   2
   How Have Environmental Management Standards and Codes
   Evolved?   9

Chapter 2
**What Is the History of ISO and the ISO 14000
Environmental Management Standards?**   13

   What Is ISO?   13
   What Is ISO's Mission?   14
   What Is the History of the ISO 14000 Standards?   15
   What Is TC 207, and How Does ISO Develop Standards?   16
   How Is ISO 14000 Structured?   18

Chapter 3
Who Can Participate in ISO 14000 Development?   21

   Why Bother Implementing an ISO 14001-Based Environmental
   Management System?   21
   What Standards Are Included in ISO 14000?   25

Chapter 4
How Do the ISO 14000 Series Standards Fit Together?   31

Chapter 5
**What Is the ISO 14001 Environmental Management System
Standard?**   33

   What Are the Elements of ISO 14001?   34

How Do I Begin Developing and Implementing an
Environmental Management System?   39
What Is the Relationship between ISO 14001 and Other
Environmental Management System Standards and Codes?   44
What Is the Relationship to Industry Standards Such as CMA
Responsible Care® and API STEP®?   44
Common Questions about ISO 14000 Registration   47
Typical Case Histories of Successfully Implemented
Environmental Management Systems   50

Chapter 6
What Is the ISO 14001 Registration Process?   53

What Steps Are Involved in Obtaining ISO 14001 Registration?   53
Should an Organization Use a Different Registrar for ISO
14001 Than It Would for ISO 9000?   54
What Is the Relationship between ISO 14000 and ISO 9000
Standards?   55

Glossary   59

Key Organizations and Contacts for More Information   67

x

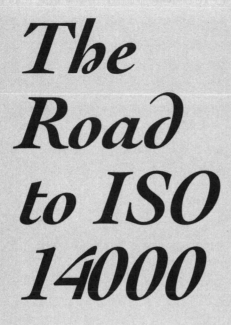

The Road to ISO 14000

Chapter 1
Introduction

The Road to ISO 14000 is intended to help environmental and business managers understand the emerging ISO 14000 series of environmental management standards. This book provides answers to the following questions:

- Why have environmental management standards been developed?
- What is the International Organization for Standardization (ISO)?
- How are ISO international standards such as ISO 14000 developed?
- Why will the ISO 14000 series of environmental management standards become globally recognized?
- What areas do the ISO 14000 environmental standards cover?
- Which ISO 14000 environmental standards are relevant to which organizations?
- What are the essential elements of the ISO 14001 environmental management systems standard?
- What are the implications of ISO 14001 for industry, and how do these standards relate to other standards and environmental compliance requirements?
- What are reasons for pursuing third-party registration or self-certification?

- What pitfalls should an organization avoid when implementing ISO 14001?
- Why should an organization implement ISO 14001?

This book does not cover the inner workings of the ISO technical committees charged with developing the ISO 14000 series of standards, nor does it provide exhaustive details about the standards. Rather, it is intended as a broad overview of the ISO 14000 standards and how they can be feasibly adopted within a competitive organization. This book provides a perspective on the implications for industries and organizations involved in environmental management issues.

2

Why Is There a Need to Develop National and International Environmental Management Standards?

National and international standards organizations have developed many voluntary, consensus-based environmental management standards and codes of practice. Standards and codes of practice have also been developed by industrial trade associations and government regulatory agencies. The primary reasons behind this trend are as follows.

1. *The increasing costs of regulatory, customer, and other stakeholder environmental performance compli-*

ance requirements. Industry is spending an esti-mated $300 billion globally on environmental protection. Major market segments that benefit from this spending include

- Consulting/engineering and design services.
- Laboratory services.
- Legal and other professional services.
- Site remediation and cleanup-related services.
- Information management and communications services.
- Pollution control equipment companies and construction companies.
- Waste treatment, storage, transportation, and disposal services.
- Companies providing treatment-, storage-, and disposal-related services.

In the U.S. market alone, annual environment-related spending is about $150 billion. Experts predict that environmental spending will approach 3 percent of the gross domestic product by the year 2000. The increasing cost of environmental compliance has particularly affected the process and natural resource industries. The Chemical Manufacturers' Association (CMA) estimates that environment compliance-related requirements, in addition to remediation spending, now average 15 percent of capital and 5 to 10 percent of operating expenses. Environmental compliance costs are similar for petroleum,

3

petrochemicals, paper products, metals, glass, and other primary raw material industries. These high compliance costs, along with an increasingly competitive global marketplace, have accelerated the interest cost-effective environmental management programs.

While it may not reduce these costs, ISO 14000 will provide a common framework for environmental costs, which will result in an equalization of environmental costs borne by competing companies in different countries.

2. *Industry now seeks to proactively improve environmental performance through self-initiatives rather than reacting to external governmental and customer requirements.* Companies no longer consider environmental compliance and remedial site cleanup as just the "cost of doing business." Managing these costs has become an important part of a comprehensive, overall business strategy.

Efforts to minimize waste and to redesign processes, products, and packaging to prevent pollution are all part of this new philosophy. *Pollution prevention* through substitution and process redesign is now considered a more acceptable environmental management solution than end-of-the-pipe waste treatment. Companies must now integrate activities such as environmental planning, program implementation, and measurement into the same overall process used

4

to manage all business activities. A growing number of companies realize that environmental activities cannot remain a staff responsibility, a lesson only recently learned by quality management professionals. Environmental protection, like quality system management, must be integrated into daily business operations.

ISO 14000 provides a framework for creating and maintaining proactive environmental programs based on self-initiatives.

3.   *Companies are discovering the economic rewards and public relations value inherent in proactive approaches to environmental management.* Products that are environmentally friendly may have greater marketplace appeal and help customers achieve their own environmental objectives more effectively. For example, more than 90 percent of the total environmental burden associated with cars, refrigerators, and washing machines is directly traceable to energy consumption during consumer use. Those companies that improve the products' energy efficiency, design, recyclable product components, and other nonpolluting manufacturing systems that address the legitimate environmental concerns expressed by customers will be tomorrow's market leaders.

Case studies presented later in this book demonstrate that proactive environmental management makes good business sense. Companies using integrated environmental management programs have realized competitive advantage and have reduced internal costs. Other companies, motivated by these success stories, are seeking to find the same process improvements. A well-designed environmental management system allows an organization to integrate environmental considerations into every aspect of day-to-day operations. Companies investing in environmental management system development take important steps toward cost reductions and leading the marketplace in breakthrough product designs.

4. *Organizations operating internationally are searching for ways to standardize often conflicting and redundant regulatory requirements, community expectations, and implementation requirements.* Increasingly, companies are marketing and distributing products and services internationally. Tracking and complying with all applicable environmental laws is a significant challenge. Environmental regulations often are more stringent in one country than in another.

Trade barriers and other inequities directly linked to meeting multiple environmental compliance requirements are a major issue in the new global marketplace. Concern that the current international patchwork of environmental compliance requirements will impede trade between nations was one of the primary drivers behind the development of ISO 14000. Industry support for these standards is a testament both to these trade concerns and to the growing acceptance of international voluntary standards.

The stated desire of the European Union (EU) to develop a single environmental management and auditing scheme for use among its member states has also driven the development of ISO 14000. The EU scheme, known as the Eco-Management and Audit Scheme/Regulation (EMAS/EMAR), is still under development, but ISO 14001 is expected to be an acceptable standard for meeting the EMS requirements of EMAS. ISO 14000 standard developers also hope that a single, internationally accepted standard will eliminate a proliferation of country-specific environmental management standards such as the British Standard Institute's 7750 (BS 7750).

5. *Stakeholders are pressuring industry to show tangible environmental performance improvements.* Today's stakeholders are more educated about environmental issues. These stakeholders include residents living near manufacturing facilities, customers, and the investment community. Environmental policy can be significantly influenced by this group of stakeholders. Implementing environmental management systems that protect the environment is an appropriate and ultimately cost-saving response.

Companies seeking proof that proactive environmental management programs deliver real marketplace benefits need look no further than their neighborhood McDonald's restaurant. During the 1980s, McDonald's was criticized for the quantities of packaging used in its restaurants. McDonald's agreed to implement aggressive efforts to redesign its packaging as part of a legal settlement with the Environmental Defense Fund. The fast-food giant reduced the volume of solid waste it generated by over 10 million pounds per year. The company identified another 35 to 40 million pounds of additional waste reduction opportunities. This campaign not only helped to create a positive environmental image for the company but also reduced its direct business costs. ISO 14000 certification will help to assure stakeholders that a company is being environmentally responsible.

6.   *Industry is focusing on expanding cost control and quality management initiatives into environmental management.* Many companies have discovered that total quality management (TQM) and similar quality management initiatives such as ISO 9000 have increased product performance, enhanced customer satisfaction, and assisted in managing costs. International quality management standards, particularly the ISO 9000 series, have had a significant operational impact on thousands of companies around the world. Qual-

ity management is no longer defined as an inspection program at the end of the production line. Implementation of ISO 9000 has resulted in improvements in financial performance, profits, and market share gain.

Government and private industry have also recognized the value of ISO 9000 and have incorporated the standard into a variety of private and public sector standards. For example, the U.S. automotive industry has incorporated the ISO 9001 standard into a single quality management system used by all three major U.S. car manufacturers and several truck manufacturers. The consolidated quality management program, known as QS-9000, is expected to become the de facto quality management standard for suppliers to these manufacturers.

ISO 9001/9002 and ISO 14001 share many common management principles. Implementation of standardized environmental management systems should deliver similar cost and efficiency rewards to companies.

How Have Environmental Management Standards and Codes Evolved?

The growing acceptance of volunteer, consensus-based quality and environmental management systems is part of an international trend toward

FIGURE 1

Trends toward International Standards

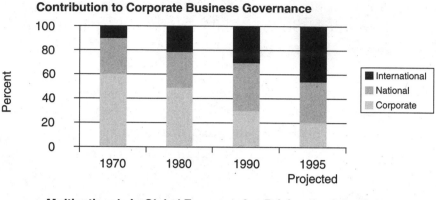

Contribution to Corporate Business Governance

**Multinationals in Global Economy Are Driving the Adoption
of International Business Standards**

Source: Adapted from Fortune, June 1992.

the use of these standards (see Figure 1). Global
standards are used in a variety of key industries,
including

- Telecommunications.
- Consumer electronics.
- Computers.
- Information management.
- Investment banking.
- Shipping/packaging systems.
- Commercial airlines operations/traffic control.
- Maritime operations.
- Product labeling.

Approximately 45 percent of governance requirements used by multinational companies are based on international standards.

Europe has taken a leadership position in the development of environmental management standards. A voluntary environmental management standard, designated as BS 7750, was first published by the British Standards Institute (BSI) in 1991. Other industry groups have also responded to stakeholder pressures to improve environmental performance by developing industry codes of performance.

Even the international business and political community has adopted a code of responsible environmental management principles. In 1991, a United Nations–sponsored sustainable development conference called for internationally recognized environmental practices. The conference published a document known as the International Chamber of Commerce Sustainable Development Charter (ICC Sustainable Development Charter). Over 3000 of the world's leading corporations have formally adopted the ICC Sustainable Development Charter.

These and other environmental standards share many elements and requirements. However, ISO 14000 may prove to be the only standard able to provide a flexible, internationally recognized

11

framework for environmental management that will address the issue of costly and duplicative regulatory and customer requirements.

Chapter 2
What Is the History of ISO and the ISO 14000 Environmental Management Standards?

What Is ISO?

The International Organization for Standardization (ISO) is a worldwide federation of national standards bodies from approximately 100 countries. ISO was established in Geneva, Switzerland, in 1946 to develop a common set of manufacturing, trade, and communications standards.

Standards published by ISO are voluntary. No legal requirements force countries or affected organizations to adopt the standards. Some industries, however, have adopted ISO standards as process and product formal requirements.

The process of standards development often takes years. Governments, affected industries, and other interested parties all participate through an international network of technical committees, subcommittees, and working groups. There are approximately 120 ISO member countries (including over 50 participating in ISO

14000 development), and more than 200 formal technical committee groups are currently at work around the world, drafting new product and process standards and updating existing ones.

The ISO can be contacted as follows:

1, rue de Varembè
Case postale 56
CH-1211 Genève 20
Switzerland
Telephone: + 41 22 749 01 11
Fax: + 41 22 733 34 30
Telex: 41 22 05 iso ch
Telegram: isorganiz
E-mail: central@isocs.iso.ch

What Is ISO's Mission?

The mission of ISO is to develop and publish standards that promote the international exchange of goods and services and develop intellectual, scientific, technological, and economic cooperation. Each country participating in ISO appoints a single body to represent its interest. The U.S. representative to ISO is the American National Standards Institute (ANSI). Contact ANSI as follows:

11 West 42nd Street
New York, NY 10036
Telephone: 212-642-4900
Fax: 212-642-0023
E-mail: sbose@ansi.org; bmarks@ansi.org; or
mhoynes@ansi.org

What Is the History of the ISO 14000 Standards?

In 1991, a panel of experts from ISO member countries formed the Strategic Advisory Group on the Environment (SAGE) to analyze global environmental trends. SAGE's task was to determine whether a set of common environmental management standards could serve to

1. Promote a common approach to environmental management similar to quality management.
2. Enhance a company's ability to measure improvements in environmental performance.
3. Facilitate trade and remove trade barriers.

SAGE's work was prompted in part by the success of the ISO 9000 quality management standards and by the national and international trends summarized in the preceding sections. These marketplace trends include the following:

- The development of global trading, led by multinational corporations.
- The introduction of sustainable development concepts by the global environmental movement.
- The proliferation of national and international legislative and regulatory requirements.

15

In the fall of 1992, SAGE recommended the development of an international set of environmental standards. A new ISO Technical Committee (TC 207) was formed in 1993 to develop these standards, now known as ISO 14000.

What Is TC 207, and How Does ISO Develop Standards?

International standards are developed in a highly structured environment consisting of subcommittees (SCs) and working groups (WGs) charged with developing specific parts of a standard. In the case of the ISO 14000 standard, more than 50 countries participate in seven subcommittees representing industry, nonprofit organizations, and government. Each subcommittee works on a specific part of the ISO 14000 standard. The seven subcommittees contain working groups, each responsible for developing a portion of the work assigned to its full subcommittee. For example, the Environmental Management Systems subcommittee (SC 1) has 3 working groups working on Environmental Management Systems, specifications, and general guidelines (see Figure 2A).

In addition to the standards development work done on the international level, individual countries form Technical Advisory Groups (TAGS). The TAG delegations allow a large group of government and private industry representatives

FIGURE 2A

Structure of TC 207

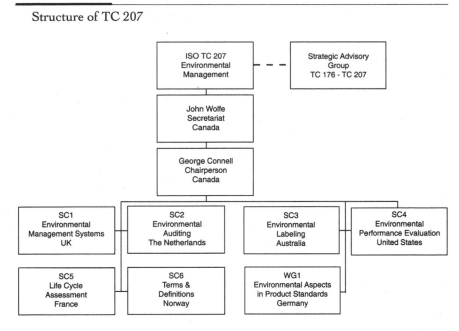

FIGURE 2B

Structure of U.S. TAG Delegation to TC 207

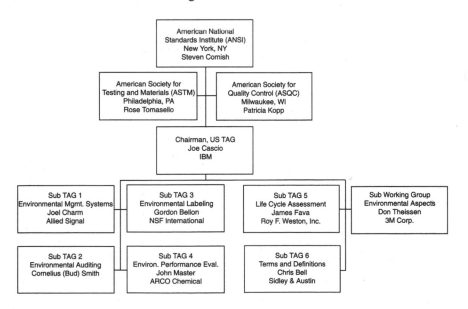

from each participating country to have a voice in the process. The U.S. TAG to the full TC 207 committee has more than 350 members. (See Figure 2B.)

A proposed ISO standard must first make its way through this committee system and be approved by the full TC 207 and TAG membership through a series of ballots before it can be published. The first of these balloting exercises allows a standard to move from a Committee Draft (CD) to a draft international standard (DIS). The ISO 14000 standard is currently a DIS. At least two-thirds of the participating TAG members must recommend ratification of a DIS before it can be published as an international standard. ISO 14001 is expected to be published as an international standard by the fall of 1996.

How Is ISO 14000 Structured?

The ISO 14000 series of standards falls into two broad categories (see Figure 3). Three of the standards focus on a company's environmental and business management system. A second series of standards, life cycle assessment and environmental labeling, focus on the product development process. The Environmental Management System Specification Standard, ISO 14001, has auditable requirements that can be

FIGURE 3

Environmental Management Areas under Development

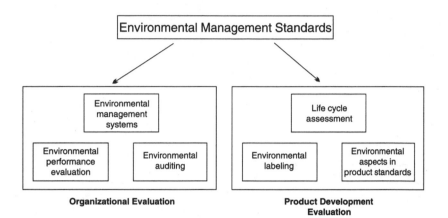

objectively assessed by a third-party accredited registrar. The remaining ISO 14000 standards are deemed as providing additional guidance.

19

Chapter 3

Who Can Participate in ISO 14000 Development?

Participation in ISO 14000 development is open to any interested individual or organization. In the United States, the American Society for Testing and Materials (ASTM) administers the process of membership application. The cost of joining the TC 207 U.S. TAG committee is $250. For information on how to join, contact

American Society for Testing and Materials
100 Barr Harbor Drive
West Conshohocken, PA 19428-2959
Telephone: 610-832-9725
Fax: 610-832-9555
E-mail: service@local.astm.org
Administrator: Rose Tomasello

Why Bother Implementing an ISO 14001-Based Environmental Management System?

Three principal factors are driving the interest in an ISO 14001-based environmental management system.

Marketplace and Customer Demands

Product performance, cost, ease of use, and quality are the traditional first-tier factors in purchasing decisions. Environmental performance is emerging as an important second-tier factor (affecting purchase decisions), especially when first-tier performance among competitive products is similar. However, environmental performance as measured by federal regulations and compliance self-declaration statements are no longer considered the best answer to pollution control and prevention. Often government command and control programs are too complex and fail to provide the most cost-effective and efficient solution. Many stakeholders view self-declaration statements with skepticism. Individual supplier audits are impractical and expensive.

The search for a low-cost and effective method for conducting supplier audits has given ISO 14000 a strong position in the marketplace. Customers will inevitably require suppliers to show environmental performance leadership. Third-party certification to ISO 14001 may well be the baseline standard that will meet these customer environmental performance requirements. ISO 14001 registration may also receive a marketplace boost by individual companies and industry sectors seeking savings and a marketplace leadership.

Operational Excellence Drivers

Implementing an environmental management system is a sound business decision. Reducing environmental impact also lowers handling and waste treatment costs and increases operational efficiency. New efficiencies gained through implementing an environmental management system provide competitive advantages and can help create superior and creative corporate cultures. Employees of environmental leadership companies often enhance a company's image through strong external community support of its environmental management programs.

The U.S. laundry detergent industry provides an excellent example. Substitution of non-phosphate-based detergent builders, more concentrated formulations, new packaging designs with refill pouches, and new low-temperature formulations changed the competitive landscape in this market sector. The net result was a new line of environmentally superior products that cost the consumer less and improved the bottom-line performance of these companies.

Compliance Drivers

Environmental regulatory bodies as well as regulated organizations are seeking more efficient programs to monitor and improve environmental performance. The ISO 14001 EMS standard and other ISO 14000 guidance standards may be chosen for this role. The U.S. Environmental Protection Agency (EPA) and many individual states understand the limitations of the current "command and control" compliance system. They are exploring whether the ISO 14001 EMS standard can be used as a voluntary program to allow companies to achieve "beyond compliance" performance as well as better pollution prevention results. This evaluation is currently being conducted by the EPA through pilot initiatives such as XL, with other pilot initiatives expected soon in states such as Pennsylvania, Illinois, and California. The objectives of these pilots is to demonstrate that superior performance can be achieved through ISO 14001 with less enforcement resources.

ISO 14001 EMS elements are also consistent with the Department of Justice Draft Sentencing Guidelines, described as mitigating factors to be considered in reducing penalties and sanctions. ISO 14001 also contains many of the mandatory EMS requirements being incorporated into recent EPA administrative orders and consent decrees, which are being negotiated to resolve enforcement actions.

The European Union (EU) is also driving acceptance of ISO 14001. Companies required to comply with the EU Eco-Management and Auditing Regulation (EMAR) may be able to use a third party–certified ISO 14001 EMS as an equivalent standard to meet the EMAR requirements. Thus, multinationals that implement an ISO 14001 EMS may be able to develop a uniform program that can meet EMAR as well as other international requirements with no additional effort. The EU decision to formalize such a program is expected sometime in 1996. Some countries (such as Taiwan) have even indicated that ISO 14001 will be a requirement for doing business with those countries.

What Standards Are Included in ISO 14000?

In a broad sense, the ISO 14000 series is defined as a systematic approach to meeting environmental obligations. The standards are designed to help a company manage and evaluate the environmental effectiveness of its activities, operations, products, and services. The ISO 14000 series includes six main topical areas:

1. Environmental management systems.
2. Environmental auditing.
3. Environmental labeling.
4. Environmental performance evaluation.
5. Life cycle assessment.
6. Environmental aspects in product standards.

Environmental Management Systems

The environmental management framework should identify resources for developing, implementing, measuring, and periodically reviewing a company's progress toward achieving the principles set forth in its mission statement and environmental policy. This framework should include a company's

- Organizational structure.
- Planning activities.
- Defined responsibilities.
- Standard practices, procedures, and processes.

Standard	Title	Scope
ISO 14001	Environmental Management Systems Specification	Formulation of environmental policy and objectives based on legislative/regulatory requirements and environmental aspects and impacts
ISO 14004	General Guidelines on Principles, Systems, and Supporting Techniques	A guide for the development and implementation of environmental management systems and principles

Environmental Auditing

Environmental auditing standards provide

- General principles of environmental auditing.
- Guidelines for auditing environmental management systems.
- Qualification criteria for environmental auditors.

Audits are an essential element of an effective environmental management system. Qualified individuals should assess

- Conformance with company and regulatory requirements.
- Progress toward achieving pollution prevention targets and objectives.

Standard	Title	Scope
ISO 14010	Guidelines for Environmental Auditing—General Guidelines on Principles, Systems, and Supporting Techniques	Provides general principles for all types of environmental auditing
ISO 14011/1	Guidelines for Environmental Auditing—Auditing Procedures—Auditing for Environmental Management Systems	Establishes audit procedures for planning and performing an environmental audit
ISO 14012	Guidelines for Environmental Auditing—Qualification Criteria for Environmental Auditors	Provides qualification criteria guidance for environmental auditors

Environmental Labeling

Environmental labeling provides guidance for three types of labels:

- Seal of approval.
- Single-claim labels.
- The environmental report card.

The standard seeks to harmonize labeling criteria and includes guidelines on environmental claims and label content.

Standard	Title	Scope
ISO 14020	Goal and Principles of All Environmental Labeling	Provides guidance used in the label drafting process.
ISO 14021	Terms and Definitions for Self-Declaration Environmental Claims	Provides guidelines for environmental claims on goods and services
ISO 14024	Environmental Labeling— Guiding Principles, Practices, and Criteria for Multiple Criteria-Based Practitioner Programs	Provides evaluation criteria for awarding labels on products and services

27

Environmental Performance Evaluation

Environmental performance evaluation (EPE) seeks to measure, analyze, assess, and describe an organization's environmental performance. EPE is used primarily to assess progress toward meeting environmental objectives and targets, especially those associated with pollution prevention. EPE is an essential continuous improvement tool in ISO 14001; it is a concept borrowed from TQM and other quality/continuous improvement standards.

Standard	Title	Scope
ISO 14031	Evaluation of the Environmental Performance of the Management Systems and Its Relationship to the Environment	Defines environmental management systems performance and provides implementation guidance
ISO 1403x	Evaluation of the Environmental Performance of the Operational Systems and Its Relationship to the Environment	Defines environmental operational performance aspects and provides implementation guidance

Life Cycle Assessment

Life cycle assessment (LCA) is a tool for evaluating the environmental attributes, burdens, and impacts associated with a product, process, or service. LCA measures the environmental impact of a product from raw material extraction to final disposal. It includes the impact of manufacturing, distribution, and transportation; product use; and recycling. LCA is used in the development of eco-labeling criteria and environmentally superior products and services.

Standard	Title	Scope
ISO 14040	Life Cycle Assessment—Principles and Guidelines	Provides a systematic set of procedures for compiling and examining environmental effects of a product or service, including materials and energy use
ISO 14041	Life Cycle Assessment—Goal and Definition/Scope and Inventory Analysis	Specifies guidelines and requirements to formulate life cycle assessment and inventory analysis
ISO 14042	Life Cycle Assessment—Impact Assessment	Proposes possible categories for an LCA impact assessment
ISO 14043	Life Cycle Assessment—Improvement Assessment	The basic content of this standard has still not been defined

Environmental Aspects in Product Standards

The area of environmental aspects in products and standards is intended to raise awareness among standard writers and designers that product design can affect the environment. The standard encourages companies to use recognized scientific methodologies that incorporate a product's life cycle in the design-making process. The standard also incorporates many current "design for the environment" methodologies.

29

Standard	Title	Scope
ISO 14060	Guide for the Inclusion of Environmental Aspects in Product Standards	Establishes general product development criteria that will reduce environmental effects

Chapter 4
How Do the ISO 14000 Series Standards Fit Together?

The ISO 14001 environmental management standard is the management framework for systematically meeting environmental obligations (see Figure 4). All of the other standards relate to ISO 14001, including self-imposed company requirements. The standard also fits well with

FIGURE 4

How Standards Plug into an ISO 14001 Environmental Management System

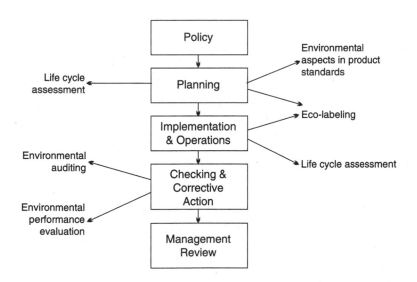

existing environmental management programs such as the CMA Responsible Care (Principles and Codes of Practice). The ISO 14001 EMS standard is expected to be published as an international standard by the end of 1996.

Chapter 5

What Is the ISO 14001 Environmental Management System Standard?

ISO 14001 is a management framework for planning, developing, and implementing environmental strategies and related programs in an organization. This framework includes the following:

- A policy that states a commitment to a specified level of environmental performance.
- A planning process and strategy for meeting this stated performance commitment.
- An organizational structure for executing the strategy.
- Specific objectives and targets.
- Specific implementation programs and related support tools to assist in meeting these stated objectives.
- Communications and training programs to execute the policy commitment.
- Measurement and review processes to monitor progress.

ISO 14001 can be used by any organization, regardless of size or business type, to develop and implement a formalized management process to improve environmental performance. ISO 14001 draws its core elements from proven management systems such as the ISO 9000 quality management series. It uses management concepts such as management by objectives, organizational development models, and continuous improvement to measure, review, perform root-cause analysis, and take corrective action. A more detailed comparison between ISO 14001 and the ISO 9000 series is made in a later section.

What Are the Elements of ISO 14001?

Management Commitment and Environmental Policy

The most senior level of the organization must do the following:

- Commit to a specific level of environmental performance appropriate to its activities, products, and services.
- Issue a policy statement that includes a commitment to pollution prevention and continuous improvement.
- Set objectives and targets within its policy statement that commit it to meeting environmental legislative and regulatory requirements.

Planning

The organization must establish and maintain processes to accomplish the following:

- Identify, evaluate, and manage environmental aspects and impacts of the company's operations, products, and services.
- Identify legal and other internally imposed requirements. Organizations usually fulfill this requirement when considering environmental aspects and objectives.
- Identify environmental performance objectives and targets for each relevant function within the company as stated in the environmental policy. Planning must also include a commitment to pollution prevention. When establishing environmental objectives, the organization should consider significant environmental aspects, relevant legal requirements, technological and financial aspects, business requirements, and stakeholders' views.
- Identify environmental management plans and programs to achieve the company's stated objectives and targets.

Implementation Operations

To effectively implement an environmental management program, an organization must do the following:

- Define, document, and communicate the organizational structure as well as the roles, responsibilities, and authority of all participants. Adequate human, technological, and financial resources must be also be

35

directed toward implementation. An appointed senior management representative must be assigned to oversee and review implementation progress.

- Ensure that all employees have the awareness and skills training needed to successfully execute their assigned roles in the implementation process.

- Establish a system to communicate internally and externally the requirements and expectations imposed by the environmental management system. The system should include a mechanism to receive and act on communications from outside parties.

- Document and record performance expectations and operating procedures, as well as record actual performance data. This information, along with legally required documentation, must be available for inspection.

- Establish and maintain a document control and archival system that meets both internal and legal requirements.

- Establish operation controls that identify, plan, implement, and maintain environmental requirements and procedures. The plan should integrate these activities into day-to-day business operations and expectations that are consistent with the company's environmental policies and objectives.

- Establish an adequate emergency preparedness and response program and periodically test it for effectiveness.

Checking and Corrective Action

Continuous improvement process requirements in ISO 14001 are met by measuring and evaluating implementation performance and effectiveness. The process is key to ensuring that a company is performing in accordance with stated policies and objectives. The principal steps in this process are as follows:

- Monitoring and measuring the effectiveness of environmental management activities.
- Correcting and preventing areas of nonconformance.
- Maintaining training, auditing, and review records.
- Performing environmental management system audits.

37

Management Review

Senior management must periodically review the environmental management system to ensure its adequacy and effectiveness. Any nonconformance must be corrected and preventive action taken. The model for connecting the elements of ISO 14001 to form an organized framework appears in Figure 5.

FIGURE 5

Environmental Management System Framework

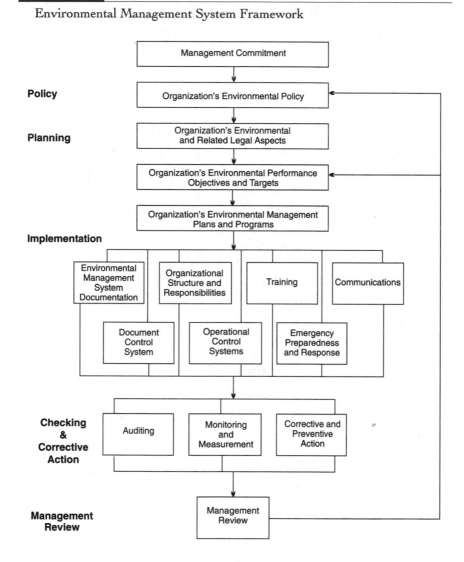

A successful ISO 14001 management framework links the company's policy requirements and objectives. If the policy states that the organization is committed to reducing its environmental impact, environmental performance targets, implementation programs, and measurement and monitoring processes must be in place to meet that stated goal.

How Do I Begin Developing and Implementing an Environmental Management System?

There are two initial steps that should be taken; an initial review and development of an improvement strategy.

Initial Review

Document your current environmental management implementation processes relative to the elements of ISO 14001. The key questions are as follows:

1. Does the organization have an overall environmental management system in place? If so, how well developed is that system?
2. Is top management committed to compliance, pollution prevention, and continuous improvement?
3. Are processes in place to track, interpret, and enforce environmental statutory and regulatory requirements that apply to the organization?

4. Are the management programs and implementation tools needed to achieve compliance and other environmental performance goals in place and operating effectively?

5. Are organizational roles, responsibilities, and authority clearly defined and communicated throughout the organization?

6. Are the necessary training and education programs in place? If so, how effective are they?

7. Are the necessary environmental management documentation and operational controls in operation to ensure that policy commitments are carried out in day-to-day operations?

8. Does the organization have an established environmental audit program and methods of measuring progress against improvement objectives and targets?

Improvement Strategy

How proactively an organization decides to pursue ISO 14000 depends on its business goals and expected rewards and on competitive considerations. Business and competitive considerations will also determine whether or not a company seeks formal registration of its environmental management system by an accredited registrar.

Here are some key questions to ask when developing and implementing an environmental management system:

Business Issues:

- Is upper-level management committed to the effort?
- Are available financial and technological resources consistent with your environmental strategy?
- Is your goal to achieve performance improvement or just to get registered?
- Should you consider a pilot implementation project to demonstrate the potential benefits to your organization and gain commitment to the effort?

Implementation and Certification Issues:

- Do you need third-party registration?
- What documentation would a third-party registrar need to understand your system?
- Is the cost of achieving third-party certification worth the potential benefit in the marketplace?
- Are the legal risks of implementing an environmental management system offset by the benefits to your organization?
- Are you able to develop an accurate *environmental aspects and impacts* analysis of your organization, including legislative and regulatory requirements?
- Are available human, technological, and financial resources adequate to meet the requirements of your system?

41

Answering these questions will allow an organization to a make a decision that makes business sense. Here are general steps to use to develop and implement an environmental management system based on ISO 14000:

- Get senior management commitment.
- Conduct an initial audit of your organization's current environmental management system as measured against ISO 14001 requirements.
- Develop an implementation plan that includes improvement objectives, provides an implementation schedule, and identifies necessary resources.
- Develop and/or update your corporate environmental policy.
- Identify and quantify the environmental aspects and impacts associated with your company's activities, products, and services.
- Identify and track legal and other environmental requirements associated with your company's activities, products, and services.
- Develop objectives that reduce the environmental impact and meet legal and other environmental regulatory and policy commitments.
- Develop environmental management and implementation plans, programs, and tools.
- Set up a program to perform ongoing implementation, monitoring, management

review, and continuous improvement activities.

Figure 6 presents a model for this development and implementation process.

FIGURE 6

ISO 14001 Environmental Management System Model

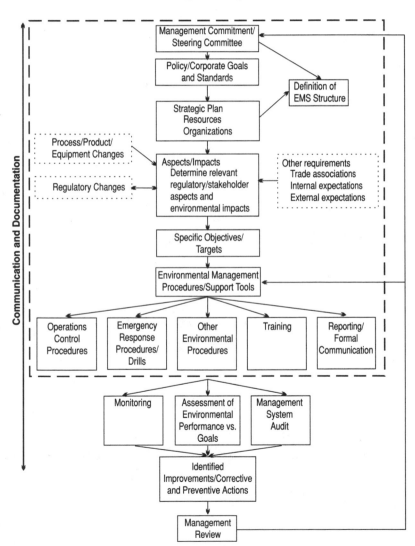

43

What Is the Relationship between ISO 14001 and Other Environmental Management System Standards and Codes?

ISO 14001, the National Sanitation Foundation (NSF) 110, the British Standards Institute's (BSI) 7750, the Eco-Management and Audit Scheme (EMAS), the International Chamber of Commerce (ICC) Sustainable Development Principles, and the Global Environmental Management Initiative (GEMI) all emphasize implementing an effective environmental management system.

ISO 14001 is unique in its ability to provide a flexible framework that can incorporate major elements covered by NSF 110, BS 7750, EMAS, and GEMI and provides for an internationally recognized third-party registration. Table 1 illustrates the elements covered by each of these standards/principles.

What Is the Relationship to Industry Standards Such as CMA Responsible Care® and API STEP®?

ISO 14001 principles are fully compatible with industry standards such as the Chemical Manufacturing Association's (CMA) Responsible Care® and the American Petroleum Institute's (API) STEP® program (see Figure 7). CMA

TABLE 1

Summary of Different EMS Systems

Environmental Management System (EMS) Elements	ISO 14001	BS 7750	EMAS	GEMI	NSF
Top management commitment	X	X	X	X	X
Initial review/assessment	X			X	
Organization mission strategy					
Environmental policy	X	X	X	X	X
Organizational roles/responsibilities	X	X	X	X	X
Environmental aspects/impacts	X	X	X	X	X
Objectives and targets	X	X	X	X	X
Identify and track requirements	X	X	X		
Compliance requirements	X	X	X	X	X
Compliance guidance		X	X	X	
Compliance programs				X	
Environmental management programs	X	X	X	X	X
Implementation programs and tools	X	X	X	X	X
Training and communication	X	X	X	X	X
Environmental records and documentation	X	X	X	X	X
Environmental performance measurement	X	X	X	X	X
Financial performance measurement					
Environmental auditing	X	X	X	X	X
Management review	X	X	X	X	X
Continuous improvement process	X	X	X	X	X
Emergency preparedness and response	X			X	X
Third-party verification	X	X	X		

45

and API standards consist of a series of explicit management principles and/or codes of practice. ISO 14001 is a broad framework for managing defined environmental commitments, objectives, and targets. ISO 14001, like other industry

FIGURE 7

Functional Comparison Matrix

Functional Areas	Standards			Codes		
	ISO 14000	BS 7750	EMAS	ICC/GEMI	Resp. Care	STEP
Environmental Management System	•	•	•			
Regulatory Compliance	•	•	•	•	•	•
Auditing	•	•	•	•		
Performance Evaluation	•	•		•		
Communications	•	•		•	•	•
Distribution	•				•	
Pollution Prevention	•	•		•	•	•
Process Safety	•			•	•	•
Health and Safety			•		•	•
Environmental Reporting	•	•	•			
Life Cycle Assessment	•					•
Emergency Response	•			•	•	
Product Label	•					•

codes, requires a company to identify all environmental aspects and impacts of its operations, products, and services. Unlike other industry codes, ISO 14001 requires a company to consider business-related risks in addition to environmental risks and legal requirements. ISO 14001 also requires formal management commitment, regular audits, and management reviews to measure performance and stimulate continuous improvement. Companies that have implemented any of these standards or codes are in a good position to begin meeting the requirements of an ISO 14001 environmental management system.

Common Questions about ISO 14000 Registration

When Should an Organization Start Adopting ISO 14001?

The key questions a company should ask before adopting the ISO 14001 standard are as follows:

- How far developed is our environmental management system?
- Is our competition pursuing ISO 14000 certification?
- Will ISO 14001 benefit our company's or division's low-cost provider or value-added competitive strategy?
- What environmental management policies or codes of practice has our industry adopted?
- Does our company export or import its products and services internationally?
- When does our company expect to achieve ISO 14000 registration? (Expect the process to take from 6 to 18 months. Companies beginning the process now could be ready for ISO 14000 certification by the time the standard is published as an international standard sometime in late 1996.)
- What are the potential costs and benefits of implementing an ISO 14001 EMS?

How Much Time Will Be Needed to Develop an ISO 14001-Compliant EMS?

The time required to implement an ISO 14001-based environmental management system depends on (1) the company's commitment to ISO 14001 implementation, (2) its available resources, (3) the current state of its environmental management system, and (4) the company's understanding of the requirements of the standard. Companies report that implementation of the BS 7750 environmental management system is a year-long process, on average. Companies that have implemented other environmental management system standards or codes spend less time preparing for the first audit, whereas companies without this background require more time to prepare for registration.

Should Your Company Seek Third-Party Registration?

48

Client requirements, business and efficiency improvements, and competitive advantage play an important part in a company's decision to seek third-party registration. Another, more practical consideration is the development of an *accreditation* body for U.S. registrars that will ultimately perform environmental audits.

Currently only two accreditation bodies, the United Kingdom Accreditation Service (UKAS) and the Raad Voor Accreditaitie (RvA) in the Netherlands, offer BS 7750 accreditation. Both UKAS and RvA are preparing to offer ISO 14001 accreditation once the standard is published. Companies already BS 7750 accredited by one or both of these bodies are expected to receive automatic accreditation for ISO 14001.

No U.S.-based accreditation body offers a similar option, but two U.S. organizations, the American National Standards Institute (ANSI) and the Registrar Accreditation Board (RAB), are developing programs to perform that service. The RAB heads up, along with its partner ANSI, the U.S. ISO 9000 registrar accreditation program. It is still questionable whether the U.S. ISO 14000 registrar accreditation program will be in place for the publication of the final standard in the fall of 1996. U.S. companies searching for registration to ISO 14000 before a national system is developed may seek out a European-based registrar.

49

What If Your Organization Needs Third-Party Registration Now?

Certification to BS 7750 achieves performance results similar to those for ISO 14001. While BS 7750 is not an officially recognized international standard, it meets many important environmental management requirements. The BSI standard is backed by an approved body of accredited registrars and a formal accreditation and registration scheme. Most BS 7750 registrars have made adjustments to the standard to make it compatible with ISO 14001.

Typical Case Histories of Successfully Implemented Environmental Management Systems

The following two cases illustrate the benefits of implementing an effective environmental management system.

CASE 1

ORGANIZATION:
Major Multinational Food and Beverage Company
SIZE:
More than 150 facilities and over $5 billion in sales/revenue per year
TYPES OF OPERATION:
Agriculture, metal product manufacturing, food and beverage, R&D and manufacturing, metal recycling
PROBLEM:
Marketing department was promoting the company as "environmentally friendly" through television advertising. Corporate management was concerned that the environmental performance of the company was not completely consistent with that advertising.
ACTIONS:
An assessment of the company's environmental management system was performed. This assessment was based on the Global Environmental Management Initiative (GEMI) and International Chamber of Commerce (ICC) principles and associated requirements for sustainable development. Both standards have similar elements contained in the proposed ISO 14001 standard. The assessment found that meeting the GEMI/ICC requirements would necessitate significant improvement

in the company's environmental management. The improvements included

- A publicly stated, proactive environmental performance policy.
- Facility-specific operating manuals delivered to the appropriate staff.
- Advanced training and skills-building programs.
- Installation of sophisticated measurement systems to be periodically reviewed by management.

The system was implemented over a two-year period beginning in the early 1990s.

RESULTS:

Net annual savings to the company (after four years) is $10 million. Savings performance continues to meet or exceed the five-year internal forecasts of approximately 45 percent. In addition, noncompliance was reduced by more than 75 percent. The company also enhanced its image as an industry leader in environmental management.

51

CASE 2

ORGANIZATION:
3M Company
SIZE:
More than 180 facilities worldwide and sales over $15 billion a year
TYPES OF OPERATION:
Plastic products manufacturing, R&D and manufacturing, paper products
APPROACH:
3M implemented an environmental program in 1975 aimed at improving the environmental quality of its operations to meet customer expectations and improve bottom-line performance. The program, known as

Pollution Prevention Pays, has been extremely successful and has achieved significant savings.

ACTIONS:

3M has implemented an integrated environmental management standard throughout the world and is currently setting up its operations to meet the requirements of ISO 14001, EMAS, and GEMI principles. The program aims to improve the quality of 3M's products, prevent pollution, and increase productivity. The program continues to seek new improvement objectives and is committed to implementation of sustainable development principles.

RESULTS:

3M found measurable benefits in efficiency and productivity by implementing an enhanced environmental management system. In 1993, the company estimated that its efforts had saved more than $60 million. 3M's cumulative savings for its Pollution Prevention Pays initiatives, based on first-year savings only, now exceed $1 billion.

What Is the ISO 14001 Registration Process?

What Steps Are Involved in Obtaining ISO 14001 Registration?

The formal ISO 14001 registration and accreditation scheme is still being developed, but the system will most likely follow the ISO 9000 and BS 7750 model. Here are the likely steps in the process:

1. Registrar and client complete an application for certification that includes confidentiality provisions.
2. Registrar reviews the existing documentation associated with the system. Often this is a simple off-site review of existing documentation.
3. Registrar conducts an on-site assessment that includes personnel interviews and a review of company records.
4. Results of the audit are presented to the company. Significant nonconformance with the standard results in a failed registration audit. After correction of nonconformances, a company may apply for a follow-up audit.
5. Most registrars conduct surveillance audits every six months. All elements of the standard are reaudited over a three-year period.

The cost of an environmental audit will most likely range from $15,000 to $25,000 per facility, depending on facility size and number of employees.

Should an Organization Use a Different Registrar for ISO 14001 Than It Would for ISO 9000?

Most organizations intend to use the same registrar for ISO 14001 that they would for ISO 9000. Some registrars are already marketing consolidated certification services. However, it is still an open question as to how rapidly ISO 9000 registrars can obtain formal accreditation and the environmental expertise needed to conduct an ISO 14000 audit. Significant economic advantages can be realized using the same registrar for both ISO 9000 and ISO 14000 audits. Some have even suggested that in the future environmental, quality, financial, operational, and other process management systems will all be certified by the same registrar.

Until the issues of registrar accreditation, audit standards, and other requirements are sorted out, companies considering either an initial ISO 9000 or ISO 14000 audit should choose a registrar carefully. Many companies with ISO 9000 experience do not have sufficient environmental expertise to properly assess companies' performance against the ISO 14001 standard. However, registrars able to offer both services can deliver the most value-added service to a company seeking dual ISO 9000/ISO 14000 registration status.

What Is the Relationship between ISO 14000 and ISO 9000 Standards?

The ISO 14000 standards draw some of their core elements from the ISO 9001/9002 Quality Management Standards. These common core elements are

- A continuous improvement management process.
- Resources and programs for effective implementation.
- Performance measurement.
- Periodic review.
- Root-cause analysis.
- Corrective action.

Section-by-section comparisons are difficult and can be misleading. Figure 8 provides a side-by-side comparison of ISO 9001 (1994) and ISO 14001 Draft International Standards. ISO 9001 requirements are far more extensive and prescriptive, whereas ISO 14001 requirements are simpler and more flexible. In addition, ISO 14001 is driven by a much larger group of formal stakeholders outside the traditional supplier/cus-

FIGURE 8

Side-by-Side Comparison of ISO 14001 and ISO 9001

1.0	**Scope**		**1.0**	**Scope**
2.0	**References**		**2.0**	**References**
3.0	**Definitions**		**3.0**	**Definitions**
4.0	**Environmental Management System Requirements**		**4.0**	**Quality Management System Requirements**
4.1	**Environmental Policy**		**4.1**	**Management Responsibility**
4.2	**Planning**		4.1.1	Quality Policy
4.2.1	Environmental Aspects		4.1.2	Organization
4.2.2	Legal and other Requirements		4.1.3	Management Review
4.2.3	Objectives and Targets		**4.2**	**Quality System**
4.2.4	Environmental Management Programs		**4.3**	**Contract Review**
4.3	**Implementation and Operations**		**4.4**	**Design Control**
			4.4.1	General
4.3.1	Structure and Responsibility		4.4.2	Design and Development Planning
4.3.2	Training, Awareness, and Competence		4.4.3	Design Input
			4.4.4	Design Output
4.3.3	Communications		4.4.5	Design Verification
4.3.4	Environmental Management System Documentation		4.4.6	Design Changes
			4.5	**Document Control**
4.3.5	Document Control		4.5.1	Document Approval and Issue
4.3.6	Operational Control		4.5.2	Document Changes and Modifications
4.3.7	Emergency Preparedness and Response		**4.6**	**Purchasing**
4.4	**Checking and Corrective Action**		4.6.1	General
			4.6.2	Assessment of Subcontractors
4.4.1	Monitoring and Measurement		4.6.3	Purchasing Data
4.4.2	Nonconformance and Corrective and Preventive Action		4.6.4	Verification of Purchased Product
4.4.3	Records		**4.7**	**Purchaser Supplied Product**
4.4.4	Environmental Management System Audits		**4.8**	**Product Identification and Traceability**
4.5	Management Review		**4.9**	**Process Control**
			4.9.1	General
			4.9.2	Special Processes
			4.10	**Inspection and Testing**
			4.10.1	Receiving Inspection and Testing

Figure continues

FIGURE 8

continued

4.10.2	In Process Inspection and Testing
4.10.3	Final Inspection and Testing
4.10.4	Inspection and Test Records
4.11	**Inspection, Measuring, and Test Equipment**
4.12	**Inspection and Test Status**
4.13	**Control of Nonconforming Product**
4.13.1	Nonconformity Review and Disposition
4.14	**Corrective Action**
4.15	**Handling, Storage, Packaging, and Delivery**
4.16	**Quality Records**
4.17	**Internal Quality Audits**
4.18	**Training**
4.19	**Servicing**
4.20	**Statistical Techniques**

57

tomer relationships that drive quality. Country-, state-, and region-specific environmental statutory and regulatory requirements must be tracked, interpreted, and implemented.

Other unique ISO 14001 requirements include

- The initial review requirement.
- Environmental aspects and impacts identification and emergency planning and response.
- A broader group of stakeholders with changing requirements.

Nevertheless, for companies that have already invested in ISO 9001 or 9002 certification, it may still make sense to consider integrating common management elements from ISO 14001 (e.g., periodic management review and organizational development programs).

Glossary

CD
Committee draft

DIS
Draft international standard

EAPS
Environmental Aspects in Product Standards

EL
Environmental labeling

EMAR
Eco-Management and Audit Regulation (European Union)

EMAS
Eco-Management and Audit Scheme (European Union)

EMS
Environmental management system

EPE
Environmental performance evaluation

LCA
Life cycle assessment

SC
Subcommittee

SubTAG
Subgroup of TAG

SWG
Subworking Group in SubTAG

TAG
Technical Advisory Group

TC
Technical Committee (TC 207 for ISO 14000)

WD
Working draft

WG
Working Group in Subcommittee

accreditation
The process or procedure by which an authoritative body, often a quasi-governmental organization, formally recognizes that a body is competent to carry out specific tasks, such as accrediting a body as qualified to register organizations as meeting ISO 14001 EMS standards.

audit

A planned, independent, and documented assessment process to determine whether agreed-upon requirements are in conformance with requirements; for example, under ISO 14001, an audit of the environmental management system.

auditor

An individual who performs an environmental audit; must meet international qualification criteria specified in the ISO 14012 standard.

certification/certified

Under ISO 14001, an assessment of an organization by an accredited body indicating that it meets the requirements of the ISO 14001 EMS standard.

61

continual improvement

Under ISO 14001, a systematic process for achieving ongoing, incremental improvements in environmental performance relative to the principles set forth in the organization's environmental policy and to the improvement objectives and targets established in the planning process.

corrective action

An action undertaken to eliminate the underlying root causes of noncompliance and other nonconformity in an organization's environmental performance.

EMS audit

A systematic and documented verification process to objectively evaluate whether the organization's EMS is functioning as intended and conforms with the principles, criteria, and goals it has committed itself to achieving.

EMS audit criteria

Under ISO 14001, criteria that encompass requirements contained in or derived from the environmental policy, objectives and targets, programs, procedures, practices, and other elements that the organization has adopted.

environment

Under ISO 14001, the surroundings in which an organization conducts its operations and distributes and sells its products and services, including air, water, land, natural resources, flora, fauna, humans, and resultant interactions, extending from the organization's local surroundings to the global context.

environmental aspects and impacts

Aspects are the specific elements of an organization's activities, operations, products, and services that interact with the environment; *impacts* are changes that result from these interactions, whether detrimental or beneficial and whether wholly or partially caused by the organization's activities, operations, products, or services.

environmental audit

A systematic, documented process for evaluating whether the organization is conforming with specified environmental requirements, including whether or not elements of the environmental management systems are in place and functioning and statutory/regulatory compliance requirements are being met.

environmental management

Under ISO 14001, the overall management function and process an organization uses to develop, implement, check, review, and maintain its environmental commitments as set forth in the environmental policy.

environmental management system (EMS)

The application of the total quality management model to environmental management; includes the various planning and organizational development activities, programs, procedures, and practices, including performance support and information management tools, and performance measurement and periodic review processes for developing, implementing, and maintaining effective environmental management in the organization.

environmental objectives and targets

Objectives are the overall environmental goals the organization has committed itself to achieving, arising from the organization's envi-

63

ronmental policy and significant environmental aspects/impacts of its activities, operations, products, and services; *targets* are detailed and quantified performance requirements and short-term goals that need to be set and met to achieve the organization's long-term environmental objectives.

environmental performance

Measurable, quantitative outputs and indicators based on environmental policy, objectives, and targets needed to monitor the impact of the organization's activities, operations, products, and services on the environment.

environmental policy

A statement of the organization's environmental philosophy, principles, and commitments to environmental performance that provides the framework for setting its environmental requirements, objectives, and targets.

interested parties

Individuals or groups concerned with or affected by the organization's environmental performance (see *stakeholders*).

life cycle

Consecutive and interconnected phases of a product or service system value chain, beginning with raw material acquisition or service system inputs and continuing through product manufacturing, distribution, use, and post-use disposition or service system outputs.

life cycle assessment

A systematic methodology for evaluating material and energy inputs and outputs and associated environmental burdens and impacts attributable to the product or service system throughout its life cycle.

nonconformance

Failure to meet or fulfill a specific requirement.

organization

In the context of ISO 14001, a company, firm, enterprise, association, or operational part thereof, regardless of whether it is incorporated, profit or not-for-profit, or public or private.

prevention of pollution (pollution prevention)

The design and use of processes, services, practices, products, and energy that avoid or minimize the creation of wastes and impacts on the environment.

product

Goods or services for consumer, commercial, or industrial purposes.

registration

A formal process during which an authorized or accredited body audits a supplier's process and verifies that a defined set of performance characteristics have been met. Companies are registered to the ISO 9000 and ISO 14000 series of standards after successfully passing a registration audit.

Responsible Care®

A comprehensive set of environmental principles and operating practices adopted by the U.S. Chemical Manufacturers Association (CMA).

root cause

The fundamental deficiency that is the cause of a nonconformance or system breakdown and must be corrected to prevent a recurrence.

root-cause analysis

A series of techniques and methodologies for identifying the root cause of nonconformances.

stakeholder

In the ISO 14001 context, a person, organization, or group that has a specific interest in an organization's EMS and environmental performance; stakeholders include employees, labor unions, suppliers, customers, government regulators, shareholders/investors, residents, community and special-interest groups, contractors, subcontractors, trade groups, and so on.

Key Organizations and Contacts for More Information

Irwin Professional Publishing
11150 Main Street
Fairfax, VA 22030
Telephone: 800-353-4809
Fax: 703-591-0971

Roy F. Weston, Inc.
1 Weston Way
West Chester, PA 19380-1499
Telephone: 610-701-3657 (Glenn Nestel, Vice-President, Management Systems Division)
610-701-5026 (Joe DelRossi, Director of Marketing, Management Systems Division)
Fax: 610-701-3651

American National Standards Institute (ANSI)
U.S. Delegate to ISO/TC 207
11 West 42nd Street
New York, NY 10036
Telephone: 212-642-4900
Fax: 212-642-4969

American Society for Quality Control (ASQC)
Administrator for SubTAGs 1 and 2
611 East Wisconsin Avenue
P.O. Box 3005
Milwaukee, WI 53201
Telephone: 414-272-8575
Fax: 414-272-1734

American Society for Testing and Materials (ASTM)
Administrator for U.S. TAG
1916 Race Street
Philadelphia, PA 19103
Telephone: 215-299-5400
Fax: 215-299-2630

Thank you for choosing Irwin Professional Publishing for your business information needs. If you are part of a corporation, professional association, or government agency, consider our newest option: Irwin Professional Custom Publishing. This service helps you create customized books, manuals, and other materials from your organization's resources, select chapters of our books, or both.

Irwin Professional Publishing books are also excellent resources for training/educational programs, premiums, and incentives. For information on volume discounts or Custom Publishing, call 1-800-634-3966.

Other books of interest from Irwin Professional Publishing . . .

ISO 14000

A Guide to the New Environmental Management Standards

Tom Tibor with Ira Feldman

ISO 14000 is a complete reference of the history, background, and development of the environmental standards, and it covers auditing, labeling, performance evaluation, and life cycle assessment. Includes discussion of the implications of ISO 14000 on international trade and regulatory enforcement. (230 pages)
ISBN: 0-7863-0523-1

THE ROAD TO QUALITY

An Orientation Guide to ISO 9000

What is ISO 9000? What are the benefits of registration? How long does ISO 9000 implementation take? Here's the ideal reference for anyone needing to grasp the absolute essentials of ISO 9000. Illustrated, concise, and written in layman's terms, *The Road to Quality* is the perfect introduction to ISO 9000. (34 pages)
ISBN: 1-883337-32-1

THE ROAD TO QS-9000

Guy Hald

Explains the new automotive standards and what they mean for business and industry. Readers will gain an understanding of the requirements for suppliers and registrars as well as implementation benefits and challenges. (50 pages)
ISBN: 0-7863-0905-9

THE ISO 9000 STARTER KIT

Introducing a valuable yet value-priced kit filled with everything you need to understand basic ISO 9000 concepts and processes, including: (1) *The Road to Quality*—A "quick guide" that delivers the fundamentals of ISO 9000 in a clear, entertaining format; (2) *ISO 9000 Questions and Answers*—Offers a more detailed explanation of ISO 9000, including accreditation, emerging standards, and more; and (3) *ISO 9000 Statistical Profile*—Explores ISO 9000 registration activity and growth in North America through a series of charts, graphs, and tables.
ISBN: 0-7863-0896-6

(continued)

QUALITY SYSTEMS UPDATE NEWSLETTER
A Global ISO 9000 and ISO 14000 Information Source

Subscribe to *Quality Systems Update* (*QSU*) and you'll receive 12 issues of the monthly newsletter that has been acclaimed by thousands of quality professionals as the preeminent publication on ISO 9000 and related standards, including QS-9000 and ISO 14000. The objective, "hard news" format provides in-depth reports on the standards, showing how they are being applied and integrated worldwide. (approx. 40 pages/month)
ISBN: 1060-1821

Most publications available in bookstores and libraries everywhere.